100 QUESTIONS FOR JEHOVAH'S WITNESSES

OWEN MORGAN

PREFACE

Jehovah's Witnesses pride themselves on being absolutely correct about a few religious beliefs prevalent in mainstream Christianity. For example, Jesus didn't believe in the doctrine of Hellfire or the Trinity—Jehovah's Witnesses are correct about that. The organization has done its research.

In the spirit of accuracy and understanding, I feel it's incumbent upon me to ask why Jehovah's Witnesses haven't adapted as new manuscripts have been unearthed and people have made new historical discoveries.

Jehovah's Witnesses are given a test colloquially called "The 100 Questions" when getting baptized. The questions can be found in the back of the Organized to Do Jehovah's Will book. Similarly, I've provided 100 questions for Jehovah's Witnesses—questions that go unanswered.

Please consider these questions in the spirit in which they're offered. I have no intention of hurting feelings, agitating, or attacking. I'm simply looking for the answers. Are Jehovah's Witnesses correct? Let's start at the beginning: the Holy Name.

CHAPTER 1
WORD TRANSLATION

1. Why use a warped version of the Holy Name, Jehovah, rather than the actual Holy Name, Yahweh?

The Tetragrammaton represents God's name: YHWH. As the name passed through Germanic regions, Y's were gradually replaced with J's because of regional pronunciations. Jews pronounced it Yahweh.

Jehovah's Witnesses consider God's name holy and believe it should be used in regular worship. Shouldn't the original be used since the name is so important to them?

2. Why does the New World Translation of the Bible replace the Greek words for "God" or "Lord" with "Jehovah?"

The Tetragrammaton does not appear in Greek scriptures. The word used to refer to God was KURIOS, meaning Lord. In some cases, THEOS was used, meaning God.

3. Why do Jehovah's Witnesses pay missionaries and Bethelites

so poorly? Can't they afford to pay the missionaries and Special Pioneers a living wage for full-time work?

Jehovah's Witnesses invite Bethelites to live and work on-site at various branches. Missionaries agree to get over 32 hours of preaching per week and receive a small stipend. What do they do when they have to enter the outside workforce? Many Bethelites don't have any marketable skills. For that matter, what are they supposed to do when it's time to retire? Why doesn't the Watchtower Society at least provide a retirement account?

4. Why do Jehovah's Witnesses believe Michael the Archangel is also Jesus?

According to the Bible book of Hebrews, no angel will ever sit at God's right hand.

But to which of the angels has he ever said, "Sit at my right hand until I make your enemies a footstool for your feet?"

HEBREWS 1:13

However, the Bible says that Jesus would sit at his right hand a few chapters later.

But when Christ had offered for all time a single sacrifice for sins, "he sat down at the right hand of God," and since then has been waiting "until his enemies would be made a footstool for his feet."

HEBREWS 10:12–13

The Bible book of Romans reaffirms that Jesus will sit at the right hand of God.

Who will condemn them? Christ Jesus is the one who died, yes, more than that, the one who was raised up, who is at the right hand of God, and who also pleads for us.

ROMANS 8:34

There is even more evidence against this claim, but that should already be sufficient.

5. Why does the Watchtower Society claim that the Archangel is a single individual rather than a class of angels?

Jehovah's Witnesses' book *What Does the Bible Really Teach?* mentions Jesus as Michael the Archangel in the appendix. The section titled "Who Is Michael the Archangel?" says the following:

God's Word refers to "Michael the Archangel." (Jude 9) This term means "chief angel." Notice that Michael is called the archangel. This suggests that there is only one such angel.

However, The New World Translation of the Bible says the following in the book of Daniel:

So Michael, **one of** the chief princes, came to help me, and I left him there with the prince of the kingdom of Persia.

DANIEL 10:13, NWT

The term "archangel" literally means "chief messenger."[1] Contrary to the Watchtower Society's claims, even the New World Translation of the Bible affirms that the Chief Messenger is a class of angels, not a singular angel.

6. Why would they insert their own additional interpretation on top of the interpretation provided within the pages of the Bible?

Does the Watchtower Society realize that apocalyptic writing was a genre of the time, no different than science fiction is today?

Why do Jehovah's Witnesses re-interpret apocalyptic literature when the writings were intended for that time and place in history?

Why isn't the interpretation given *within the same story* acceptable? Should we trust the Bible or not?

CHAPTER 2
FALSE PROPHECY

**7. Why does the Watchtower Society insist that the date
Solomon's temple fell was 606 BCE rather than 586 BCE?**

An ancient tablet cataloged as VAT4956, currently on display in a Berlin Museum, tells us when it was written through star charts.[1,2] The tablet is from the 37th year of Nebuchadnezzar's reign. It provides 30 positions of the moon and five positions of the planets for us to use as a timestamp reference. By running calculations to find out when the planets and moon would be in those locations, we have a precise time for when the tablet was written.

The tablet VAT4956 shows star positions, which won't happen for thousands of years. Beyond a shadow of a doubt, the tablet reveals that the 37th year of Nebuchadnezzar's reign was in 568/567 BCE. The 37th year of Nebuchadnezzar's reign was in 567 BCE. According to Jeremiah 52:29, Solomon's Temple fell in the eighteenth year of Nebuchadnezzar's reign.

This is the number of the people whom Nebuchadnezzar took into exile: in the seventh year, three thousand and twenty-three Judeans; 29 in the eighteenth year of Nebuchadnezzar he took into exile from Jerusalem eight hundred and thirty-two persons.

JEREMIAH 52:28–29

Since his 37th year was in 568 BCE, His 18th year was in 586 BCE. Solomon's temple fell in 586 BCE.

8. Why can't Jehovah's Witnesses accept that the Bible math used to calculate the year 1914 is wrong?

Jehovah's Witnesses' calculation to arrive in 1914 is based on Solomon's Temple falling in 606 BCE. It did not fall in 606 BCE. Why won't Jehovah's Witnesses acknowledge that fact and admit that the prophecy was wrong?

9. Why do Jehovah's Witnesses believe written history has accurately kept track of weeks, months, and even years?

Does the Watchtower Society account for the fact that Jews used a completely different calendar when calculating 1914? Exactly how many years were there between 606 BCE and 1914 BCE?

The Julian calendar was instituted in 45 BCE, and the Gregorian calendar in 1582. Before the Julian calendar, the world used many different calendars. Still, the most common and famous in the Middle East was the Hebrew/Jewish calendar. The Jewish calendar worked off lunar cycles and had varying numbers of days: sometimes 353, sometimes 354, and sometimes 355.

Did Jehovah's Witnesses account for leap years in their calculations? What about leap seconds? Why do they count from 606 BCE to 1914 BCE, 2,520 years, without accounting for missing days in the year? Are we counting revolutions around the sun? If we count lunar years, why don't we count lunar years from start to finish? Where is the consistency?

10. Why do Jehovah's Witnesses accept Charles Taze Russell's Bible math about the end coming in 1914 when the same Bible math was used to fail the Millerites only 75 years earlier?

In addition to calculating 1914 based on the false premise that Solomon's Temple fell in 606 BCE rather than 586 BCE, Charles Taze Russell used another method. He measured the Pyramid of Giza using pseudo-scientific measurements called "pyramid inches," which he used in more math equations.

Jehovah's Witnesses acknowledge the pyramidology of Charles Taze Russell in a Watchtower from May 15, 1956, pp. 297–300.[3] They named each participant in forming the idea but conveniently left Charles Taze Russell out of the article.

Proof of Charles Taze Russell's involvement and belief in pyramidology can be found in his own writings. He wrote a six-part series of books titled Studies in the Scriptures. The pyramidology can be found in "Series III – *Thy Kingdom Come*, p. 338

11. Why did they leave Charles Taze Russell out of the *Watchtower* article about pyramidology?

Are they ashamed of something? Why do Jehovah's Witnesses reject his pyramidology but accept the faulty date of 606 BCE? Why is Temple math more legitimate than pyramid math? How was Charles Taze Russell divinely inspired by Bible math but not divinely inspired by pyramidology calculations?

12. Why did the Watchtower Society claim that the end would

come before the year 2000, only to reverse that position by changing the wording later?

Jehovah's Witnesses released a *Watchtower* in 1989 that prophesied the end would come before the year 2000.[4] Later, they changed the wording, but the originals can still be found.

Previous wording:

How thrilling that must have been for Paul and Barnabas—sailing to their first foreign assignment! The apostle Paul was spearheading the Christian missionary activity. He was also laying a foundation for a work that would be *completed in our 20th century*.

JEHOVAH'S WITNESSES. *THE WATCHTOWER.*
JANUARY 1, 1989. P. 12

Current wording:

… He was also laying a foundation for a work that would be *completed in our day.*

13. How can Jehovah's Witnesses be trusted to know when the end will come after falsely prophesying that it would come in the autumn of 1975?

In November 1968, a district overseer gave a talk at an assembly in Texas. In his talk, he said, "Not really a full 83 months remains, so let's be faithful and confident and … we will be alive beyond the war of Armageddon…"[5]

Countless Jehovah's Witnesses publications prophesied the end would come in the autumn of 1975. A single incorrect prophecy makes the Governing Body false prophets and invalidates their mandate to lead, according to Deuteronomy 18:22.

14. Why do Jehovah's Witnesses continue to believe that the end will come within the generation of people alive to see the events of 1914 unfold when that generation is very clearly dead and gone?

In *The Watchtower* from May 15, 1984, pp. 4–7, Jehovah's Witnesses claimed that the generation anointed before 1914 would not die off before the end came. They commonly use Fred Franz as a gauge, claiming he was anointed in 1913. Why do they ignore that he said he was anointed in 1914?

When Fred Franz died in 1992, why didn't they admit that the Second Generation teaching was wrong? Why did they change the word "generation" to mean contemporary instead? We have a word for contemporary. The word is contemporary. Generation means something completely different.

15. What will the Governing Body do when the Second Generation teaching fails?

What is the Governing Body of Jehovah's Witnesses going to do when the end doesn't come by the time the second generation has passed away? Will the Watchtower Society do what they did for their 1975 prophecy? Will they try to cover it up? Will they try to erase it from history? Why can't they admit when they get things wrong and work to correct it?

CHAPTER 3
THE LGBT COMMUNITY

16. Why did Jehovah's Witnesses claim that touching yourself would turn you gay?

Jehovah's Witnesses have had a book for young people for years. Today, it's the Young People Ask book. In the 1970s, it was titled *Your Youth: Getting the Best Out of It*. Here's what the youth book had to say on the subject of homosexuality:

In fact, masturbation can lead into homosexuality. In such instances the person, not satisfied with his lonely sexual activity, seeks a partner for mutual sex play. This happens much more frequently than you may realize. Contrary to what many persons think, homosexuals are not born that way, but their homosexual behavior is learned. And often a person gets started when very young by playing with another's sexual parts, and then engaging in homosexual acts.

JEHOVAH'S WITNESSES. *YOUR YOUTH: GETTING THE BEST OUT OF IT.* 1976, P. 39

Why did Jehovah's Witnesses release that book? Why was it used for years after its release? Why did they quietly remove that sentiment from future editions of teen books? Do they not believe it anymore? Why not explicitly retract it?

17. Why isn't the majority of the human population gay?

Masturbation is very well studied. The scientific consensus is… it's completely normal and even offers health benefits. The population of straight or bisexual men in the UK should be 4% if we believe this article from Jehovah's Witnesses and a scientific survey from 2018. A 96% rate of gay men would have surely been reported everywhere.

18. Why do Jehovah's Witnesses think that being gay is wrong?

The Bible mentions homosexuality in any form in a total of 6 out of 31,102 verses. It seems clear to me that it wasn't an important issue. Three of those verses are in the Old Testament. Genesis 19, the story of Sodom and Gomorrah, and Leviticus 18 and 20.[1,2]

Some of the verses are based on Sodom and Gomorrah, so it's important to note that those cities weren't destroyed because gay people lived within their walls.

> Now this was the sin of your sister Sodom: She and her daughters were arrogant, overfed and unconcerned; they did not help the poor and needy.
>
> *EZEKIEL 16:49*

Sodom *was* found to have rapists within its walls when they arrived to investigate the city. Still, the reason for its destruction was the ill-treatment of the poor.

Leviticus 18 and 20 were part of the old law, which was invalidated when Jesus died. That's why we eat pork and shellfish today.

Three verses can be found in the New Testament. 1 Corinthians 6:9–10, 1 Timothy 1:10, and Romans 1:26–27

> Do you not know that wrongdoers will not inherit the kingdom of God? Do not be deceived! Fornicators, idolaters, adulterers, male prostitutes, sodomites, thieves, the greedy, drunkards, revilers, robbers—none of these will inherit the kingdom of God.
>
> *1 CORINTHIANS 6:9–10*

This verse condemns male prostitutes specifically.

> ...fornicators, sodomites, slave-traders, liars, perjurers, and whatever else is contrary to the sound teaching.
>
> *1 TIMOTHY 1:10*

According to scholars who study this subject for a living, the act being condemned here was being the passive participant in the equation—that is, being a bottom.

> For this reason God gave them up to degrading passions. Their women exchanged natural intercourse for unnatural, and in the same way also the men, giving up natural intercourse with women, were consumed with passion for one another. Men committed shameless acts with men and received in their own persons the due penalty for their error.
>
> *ROMANS 1:26–27*

In addition to talking about male prostitution and/or being the passive participant in the equation, the verses also referred to pederasty. Older men would take young boys as pupils and sexually assault them regularly. That was considered a sexual sin. Being gay was not considered a sin at the time.

Paul wrote those Bible books. He converted to Christianity about three years after Jesus had already died. He never met Jesus personally. Paul's goal was to form Christian culture in its early days. For example, Paul caught wind of a man in the Corinth congregation bragging about sleeping with his stepmother. He worried that would make Christianity look bad, so he ordered them to expel him from the congregation. He reversed course in 2 Corinthians, but the point is that Paul was overly worried about image. Prostitution, pederasty, and sleeping with one's stepmother were out.

Not only did Paul never condemn long-term gay relationships, but more importantly, Jesus didn't condemn them, either. Jesus didn't say a single word about being gay. Jesus cared most about helping the poor. If you could help the poor and give his family (aka any human) something to drink when they were thirsty or eat when they were hungry, you were considered a sheep rather than a goat (Matthew 25:31–46).

19. Why do Jehovah's Witnesses add expectations for Christians on top of what Jesus outlined?

Jesus said two new commandments sum up all others: Love your neighbor as yourself and love God with your whole heart, soul, and mind (Matthew 22:37–39).

Jesus said there was one requirement to enter the kingdom of God besides those two commandments. He explained this in the sheep and goats parable in Matthew 25:31–46: "You gave me water when I was thirsty. You gave me clothes when I was naked." The sheep said, "Lord, when did we do those things for you?" Jesus said, "What you did to the least of my family, you did for me."

The message is clear: Love your neighbor as yourself. That includes caring for the poor, which was Jesus' primary focus. It had nothing to do with knocking on doors, talking to disfellowshipped family, attending a non-believing parent's funeral, or hating gay people:

> The Bible's stand is not unreasonable. It simply directs those with homosexual urges to do the same thing that is required of those with an opposite-sex attraction —to "flee from fornication." The fact is that millions of heterosexuals who wish to conform to the Bible's standards employ self-control despite any temptations they might face. Those with homosexual inclinations can do the same if they truly want to please God.[3]

20. Why do Jehovah's Witnesses avoid birthdays? The Bible doesn't say anything about Jesus celebrating them.

Then again, they hate gay people, though he didn't say anything about that either. Jehovah's Witnesses don't celebrate birthdays *because* Jesus didn't say anything about birthdays. In fact, there's no record of Jesus ever mentioning birthdays, good or bad. Jehovah's Witnesses use that as the basis for avoiding birthday celebrations:

> The Bible never refers to a servant of God celebrating a birthday. This is not simply an oversight, for it does record two birthday celebrations by those not serving God. However, both of those events are presented in a bad light.[4]

But they have a problem with gay people, even though he

didn't say anything about that either. This is yet another example of Jehovah's Witnesses unevenly applying principles.

21. Why do Jehovah's Witnesses act like they're the victims of persecution when they are the ones persecuting others?

Jehovah's Witnesses tell a story about persecution in a 2023 *Watchtower*. The story is farfetched at best, but it clearly portrays how Jehovah's Witnesses feel about gay people. The organization is desperate to convince people that they "love everybody," as they claim being gay is tantamount to child molestation. Take a look at the 2023 *Watchtower* article:

Some even try to bully our young ones into breaking their loyalty to Jehovah. Note, for example, what happened to a young man named Graeme, who lives in Australia. He faced a challenging situation when he attended high school. The teacher asked the class how they would react if a friend confided in them about being a homosexual. The teacher said that all in the class who would support a friend in pursuing such a lifestyle must stand on one side of the room; those who would not, on the other side. Graeme says, "The entire class stood on the side that supported that lifestyle except for me and another Witness." What happened next was a real test of Graeme's loyalty to Jehovah. "For the rest of the hour-long class," he says, "the other students and even the teacher taunted and insulted us. I did my best to defend my faith in a calm and reasonable way, but they didn't listen to a word I said." What effect did this test of loyalty have on Graeme? He says, "I did not like being the target of such verbal attacks, but I felt incredibly happy that I was able to defend my beliefs without compromise."

JEHOVAH'S WITNESSES. *THE WATCHTOWER.* AUGUST, 2023. P. 6

There are still many anti-gay people around. The Jehovah's Witness wouldn't be the only one to do so in this scenario.

The point of the article, though, is to make Jehovah's Witnesses feel like they're persecuted at every turn. The world is against them, and this fabricated story from the Watchtower only reinforces that perception.

CHAPTER 4
THE MANDATE OF HEAVEN

22. Are Governing Body members prophetic or not?

The Governing Body members claim to be prophets of God.

Those who do not read can hear, for God has on earth today a prophetlike organization, just as he did in the days of the early Christian congregation.

JEHOVAH'S WITNESSES. THE WATCHTOWER. OCTOBER 1, 1964, P. 601

For an answer, people should listen to the plain preaching by the remnant prefigured by Jeremiah, for these preach to men the present-day fulfillment of Jeremiah's prophecies. Who made them a prophet to speak with the authority that they claim? Well, who made Jeremiah a prophet?

JEHOVAH'S WITNESSES. THE WATCHTOWER. JANUARY 15, 1959. PP. 39–41

In part 2 of Jehovah's Witnesses' annual meeting, released January 2024, at the 44-minute mark, Governing Body member Geoffrey Jackson revealed "new light," which is what they call new doctrine that replaces or adds to existing doctrine, that people could rejoin Jehovah's Witnesses after the Great Tribulation starts. The previous position was that the metaphorical "door of the ark" would close after the Tribulation begins, and membership would be closed to everybody. Jackson said the following:

> If they change their hearts and joined us, would we be disappointed? Now, we can't be dogmatic. But, we don't want to be like Jonah.

Jonah was a prophet of God who refused to prophesy. As punishment for refusing to deliver prophetic information, he was swallowed by a big fish. By comparing themselves to Jonah, they are tacitly claiming to be prophets.

The Governing Body often claims not to be prophets. In the 2023 annual meeting, Jeffrey Winder, a member of the Governing Body, outright states that God does not inspire him in any unique way. However, the Governing Body constantly offers prophecy—1914, 1925, 1975, 2000, and the Second Generation teaching, to name a few. They talk about being prophets and offer prophecies fairly regularly—1914, 1925, 1975, 2000, and the Second Generation teaching, to name a few.

Deuteronomy Chapter 18 outlines the expectations of prophets. It says that prophets should be tested. They should be ignored and distrusted if what they say doesn't come true. What they said did not come from God.

Not only have prophecies described by the Governing Body of Jehovah's Witnesses not come true, but some have been proven false.

23. Why do Jehovah's Witnesses believe only a specific subset of Christians should follow one of Jesus' most important commands before his death?

Matthew 26 describes Jesus' final night on earth. He was with his disciples at the Last Supper. He instructed them to eat bread and drink wine in remembrance of him. The key word to note in Matthew is the word "disciple."

Apostles were leaders, but disciples were students of Jesus. In Matthew 26:26, Jesus instructs disciples to take communion.

> While they were eating, Jesus took a loaf of bread, and after blessing it he broke it, gave it to the disciples, and said, "Take, eat; this is my body." Then he took a cup, and after giving thanks he gave it to them, saying, "Drink from it, all of you; for this is my blood of the covenant, which is poured out for many for the forgiveness of sins."
>
> *MATTHEW 26:26–28*

Mark's account reaffirms that disciples were instructed to participate in the ceremony to remember Jesus.

> While they were eating, Jesus took bread, and when he had given thanks, he broke it and gave it to his disciples, saying, "Take it; this is my body." Then he took a cup, and when he had given thanks, he gave it to them, and they all drank from it.
>
> *MARK 14:22–23*

Jesus clearly stated that his disciples should do this in remembrance of him. In Luke, the scene described only included his apostles. Even so, he didn't say the observance was exclusive to leadership. It seems clear that Jesus wanted people to *remember* him. That was the point of the ceremony. Why do Jehovah's Witnesses limit who is allowed to remember Jesus by taking communion?

24. Do anointed brothers who've been jailed have to drink toilet wine for the Memorial?

Will Jehovah understand if they choose not to partake? Is it okay if they partake in their hearts, or must they drink the toilet wine in prison? Is leavened bread okay, or should they find a way to un-leaven their sandwich bread? Is yeast the issue, or is it the air?

Does Jehovah think peoples' best efforts are reasonable enough in this case? If so, why doesn't Jehovah think people's best efforts are reasonably sufficient in other areas of their lives? How can people "fall short," and who can judge whether they've fallen short, aside from Jehovah himself?

25. Geoffrey Jackson, under oath before the entire world, stated that it would be presumptuous to think Jehovah's Witnesses are God's only spokespeople. Does he truly believe that, or was he lying?

Geoffrey Jackson was called to testify in front of the Australian Royal Commission for their mishandling of child sexual abuse cases.

While testifying, the Australian Royal Commission asked Governing Body member Geoffrey Jackson the following question: "Do you see yourselves as Jehovah God's spokespeople on earth?"

Geoffrey Jackson responded, "That, I think, would certainly be quite presumptuous to say that we are the only spokesperson which God is using."

Is this an example of a Governing Body member lying under oath to avoid bad press? It's unacceptable for a Jehovah's Witness to lie to protect their own lives. Do the rules only apply to the followers but not the leaders?

26. Why do Jehovah's Witnesses use the Two Witness Rule even in heinous criminal situations from which the Two Witness Rule is specifically Biblically exempted?

Deuteronomy 22:25–27 outlines exemptions from the Two Witness Rule:

> If, however, the man happened to meet the engaged girl in the field and the man overpowered her and lay down with her, the man who lay down with her is to die by himself, and you must do nothing to the girl. The girl has not committed a sin deserving of death. This case is the same as when a man attacks his fellow man and murders him. For he happened to meet her in the field, and the engaged girl screamed, but there was no one to rescue her.

DEUTERONOMY 22:25–27

Why do Jehovah's Witnesses ignore that set of verses to the detriment of so many children within the organization?

27. Why do Jehovah's Witnesses believe the Two Witness Rule has modern-day relevance since the invention of the video camera and DNA testing?

The Bible outlines a system of governance, but society has advanced technology that renders the old method obsolete today.

Jehovah's Witnesses are not investigators. As a body, elders cannot access DNA testing, databases, or other advanced technology to solve crimes. Why, then, do Jehovah's Witnesses have a history of encouraging members of the religion to handle things internally instead of calling the police?

Why has the Watchtower Society lost so many lawsuits for their mishandling of child sexual abuse cases?

After the Governing Body recognized that more child abusers could be caught by means other than the Two Witness Rule, why did they stubbornly refuse to explicitly instruct elders to report cases of child sexual abuse to the police? Why won't they, at the very least, advise elders to instruct victims' parents to call the police? How can a system possibly be called moral when it explicitly leaves room for predators to escape justice?

28. Why was Tony Morris fired from the Governing Body?

What happened to Tony Morris? Why was he fired? He shaped a lot of doctrine while on the Governing Body. He claimed members wouldn't enter the new system if they didn't knock on doors often enough. Is that still valid? Are any of his "new light" claims still active? If so, how was it determined which parts were from Jehovah and which were from his brain?

29. Why were Tony Morris's morning worship videos removed from the Jehovah's Witness website?

Why were Tony Morris's videos removed from the website? Are his videos no longer considered spiritual food? If his messages were being given to us as spiritual food, but we found that they weren't spiritual food after all, how can we trust that we're receiving it now? Are Jehovah's Witnesses starving people's spirits?

30. Who can decide if one of the Governing Body members isn't providing spiritual food after all?

How do we know the people currently on the Governing Body have Jehovah's mandate? Maybe Tony Morris had Jehovah's Mandate, and the other Governing Body members didn't. How can we tell?

I remember a test presented to God's people in Deuteronomy 18:22. If their prophecies fail, they aren't prophets. They're liars.

CHAPTER 5
INCORRECT BELIEFS

31. Why do Jehovah's Witnesses believe that Jesus died on a stake instead of a cross?

Jehovah's Witnesses' reasoning rests upon the word used to describe it: the Greek word *stauros*. Stauros means an upright pole. However, we have descriptions of crosses used to execute people. One such description can be found in the epistle of Barnabas. In that book, it's likened to somebody standing upright with outstretched arms or like a ship's mast. It was a cross. Not a stake.[1]

Scholars universally accept that Jesus died by the cross, not by torture stake. Jehovah's Witnesses are the only ones who deny this. Bart Ehrman, for example, goes into detail about why we know it was a cross rather than a stake.

Not only does the epistle of Barnabas describe a cross, but it was *the* common method of execution at the time. It was a cross. It just was.

32. Why do Jehovah's Witnesses ignore the verse that says

multiple nails were used to hold Jesus' hands to his torture device?

John 20:25 indicates that multiple nails were used to execute Jesus. Why would multiple nails be used if his hands were crossed one over another? Were his hands comically large?

> So the other disciples told him, "We have seen the Lord!" But he said to them, "Unless I see the nail marks in his hands and put my finger where the **nails** were, and put my hand into his side, I will not believe."
>
> *JOHN 20:25*

Coupled with the fact that the cross was simply the standard method of execution at the time, the conclusion is undeniable. Jesus died by the cross, not by the stake. The Watchtower Society got downright indignant about the subject in the *Watchtower* from April 1, 1984, pp. 30–31.

> Much time and trouble have been wasted in disputing as to whether three or four nails were used in fastening the Lord. Nonnus affirms that three only were used, in which he is followed by Gregory Nazianzen. The more general belief gives four nails, an opinion which is supported at much length and by curious arguments by Curtius. Others have carried the number of nails as high as fourteen.
>
> JEHOVAH'S WITNESSES. *THE WATCHTOWER.* APRIL 1, 1984. PP. 30–31

If you notice, the last sentence uses weasel words, meaning they don't specify their source. "Others have carried the number"—

what others? Who? Which people specifically say that? Do they have the credentials to make that kind of claim? If these "others" really did claim that, why didn't Jehovah's Witnesses simply give their name like they gave the names of their other sources?

33. Why do Jehovah's Witnesses use the JW.ORG logo as an idol?

Another complaint from Jehovah's Witnesses is that the cross is used as an idol. I could agree with that assessment, but Jehovah's Witnesses use their JW.ORG logo similarly.

They use the logo on their books, pens, magazines, stickers, buttons, pins, necklaces, and even earrings. Jehovah's Witnesses might say they're just using it to advertise the religion. I would argue that Christians are just using the cross to advertise their religion, too. Some don't, certainly—but many do.

Jehovah's Witnesses lay out the argument against the cross in their *Watchtower* from November 1, 1950, pp. 425–427.

> Reference to the original languages in which the Bible was written will show beyond a question of doubt that Christ was never hung on any pagan cross. Hence, the use of the word "cross" in the English-language Bibles is a mistranslation.

The *Watchtower* quotes its own Bible translation to back up the claim. The article continues:

> On this, the New World Translation of the Christian Greek Scriptures, in its appendix, on pages 768–771, in commenting on Matthew 10:38, where the Greek word σταυρός (stau·ros') first appears and which is translated "cross" in most Bibles, states: "This is the expression used in connection with the execution of Jesus at Calvary. There is no evidence that the Greek word stau·ros' meant here a 'cross' such as the pagans used as a

religious symbol for many centuries before Christ to denote the sun-god. [sic]"

This article is still considered valid doctrine and is referenced on the Jehovah's Witness website. The article cites a publication they wrote as evidence of their claim about the cross.

34. Why do Jehovah's Witnesses cite their own literature as evidence of their claims?

If you'll notice, I haven't quoted a single publication as evidence in one of my other publications. It's circular. Why did Jehovah's Witnesses cite their own publication as evidence of their claim that the original language says "stake" instead of "cross?"

Do Jehovah's Witnesses believe that their own publications are equivalent, or even superior to the Bible? Do they think the Bible can't be understood without the assistance of the Watchtower Society's publications? This is the definition of "source: I made it up."

35. Who worked on the translation effort for The New World Translation of the Bible?

The world has no idea who translated Jehovah's Witnesses' translation of the Bible. They haven't released the names of the translators. That's a big deal within scholarly communities. If a Bible translation is released, the translators' names should be, too. I don't know of any other Bible translation that doesn't list its translators.

36. Why should we trust the organization to give us honest and complete interpretations of works they don't cite?

In many instances, Jehovah's Witness literature doesn't even name the source, let alone properly cite a source. Why should we believe a word out of the mouths of the Governing Body or the writing department when they consistently get it wrong?

37. Why do Jehovah's Witnesses bend the New World Translation to support the belief that Jesus created the world instead of God creating the world?

Jehovah's Witnesses believe that God created Jesus, and Jesus created everything else. In a way, Jesus is the actual divine creator. Here's the NRSVA translation of Colossians 1:17:

He himself is before all things, and in him all things **hold together**.

COLOSSIANS 1:17, NRSVA

Take a look at Jehovah's Witnesses version, the New World Translation:

Also, he is before all other things, and by means of him all other things **were made to exist.**

COLOSSIANS 1:17, NWT

Why did Jehovah's Witnesses translate it that way? No other major translation interpreted the language to mean that everything was "made to exist" using Jesus.

38. Why do Jehovah's Witnesses add another layer of prophecy on top of what's already described in Daniel regarding the King of the North?

Daniel, Chapter 11 is an example of a messenger explaining a fantastical vision of a King of the North and a King of the South to the writer.[2] At the time, the Ptolemaic Empire (King of the South) and the Seleucid Empire (King of the North) engaged in a vicious war, and Jerusalem was caught in the middle. The battle is widely accepted to be the sixth Syrian war.

An angel already explained the apocalyptic vision within the text. How can Jehovah's Witnesses read a text that God already interpreted through an angel and claim that there's an additional interpretation that God didn't see fit to describe in the Bible?

Why would God give a secret interpretation to the Governing Body and provide the rest of the world no way of independently verifying what they claim? Why is the angel's interpretation included at all if it isn't the correct one?

39. Why do Jehovah's Witnesses reject God's prophetic interpretation of the book of Daniel? Why do Jehovah's Witnesses think they're more qualified than Daniel to interpret the prophecy?

Daniel, Chapter 2 contains an apocalyptic vision of a statue of Nebuchadnezzar. Daniel explains that each section of the statue represents a world empire. Daniel uses the same pattern in Chapter 8 in his apocalyptic vision about beasts coming from the sea.

In Daniel, Chapter 8, an angel lists those empires as Babylon, Persia, and Greece. Then the angel says the Greek Empire will shatter into four kingdoms. That's exactly what happened. The Seleucid Empire was the kingdom that ruled over Jerusalem. In the statue prophecy from Daniel 2 and the beasts of the sea prophecy from Daniel 8, Daniel was prophesying that the Seleucid Empire would be destroyed for persecuting God's people.

After the Seleucid Empire was described as one of four broken pieces of a larger empire in Chapter 8, Daniel gives us absolutely no clues as to what the next empire will be. That's because the Roman

Empire wouldn't exist for another 100 years after the Book of Daniel was written.

The angel in Daniel 8 says the empires are Babylon, Persia, Greece, and the Seleucid Empire. Jehovah's Witnesses take an extra step to interpret prophecy beyond what the Bible explains. To Jehovah's Witnesses, the legs represent Rome instead of the Seleucid Empire, and the feet of clay and iron represent the Anglo-American Empire instead of the Roman Empire.

Why do Jehovah's Witnesses skip over the Seleucid Empire, which was next to rule Jerusalem? America has existed for as long as the Seleucid Empire: between 200 and 300 years.

40. How can Jehovah's Witnesses ignore multiple empires that came after the Roman Empire but before the Anglo-American Empire?

The Muslim world controlled modern-day Israel and Jerusalem for centuries. Even ignoring the Ottoman Empire, shouldn't Jehovah's Witnesses at least consider the other Muslim empires that came before?

41. Why do Jehovah's Witnesses believe that the British Empire was a remnant of the Roman Empire?

The *Daniel's Prophecy* book, published by the Watchtower Society, says that the Roman Empire eventually became the British Empire. This belief justifies ignoring every other empire to control Jerusalem since Jesus' day.

What makes them think the Roman Empire turned into the British Empire? The Western Roman Empire became the Byzantines, and the Eastern Roman Empire became Rome, Italy.

The belief that the Western Roman Empire eventually became the British Empire is necessary to accept Jehovah's Witnesses' interpretation of Nebuchadnezzar's statue prophecy from Daniel 2.

Suppose Jehovah's Witnesses believe the Western Roman Empire became the British Empire. Why don't they also believe that the Babylonian Empire became the Persian Empire and count both empires as the statue's golden head?

Why did Jehovah's Witnesses skip over Britain's historical rival, France, before America even existed?

42. Why do Jehovah's Witnesses believe that demons possess objects, such as Smurf dolls?

In the 1980s, an urban legend swept through congregations of Jehovah's Witnesses. It was based on the Smurfs. Jehovah's Witnesses heavily demonized the Smurfs. They didn't outright ban the TV show, but the culture controlled people more effectively than doctrinal commands ever could.

The urban legend changes from person to person, but my version describes a girl with a Smurf doll in her meeting bag. She showed up to the Kingdom Hall, and during the meeting, the Smurf doll stood up out of the purse and exited the Kingdom Hall, speaking obscenities on its way out the door. The legend claims that Jehovah's light was just too bright for it.

The urban legend seems bizarre, but Jehovah's Witnesses believe that objects can be possessed and animated by demons. It's the same reason they encourage people to be cautious about shopping at yard sales. You never know what the previous owner was up to. With those premises, is it such a leap to believe it could happen to a Smurf doll?

In recounting this myth, I've found a workaround—if you purchase something at a yard sale, simply bring it into the Kingdom Hall. If it doesn't run away swearing, it should be demon-free. Right?

43. Why don't Jehovah's Witnesses allow women to be involved in the teaching process, just like men?

1 Timothy 2:12 discusses women's involvement in the church.

> I permit no woman to teach or to have authority over a man; she is to keep silent.
>
> *1 TIMOTHY 2:12*

Jehovah's Witnesses are aware of deeply complex scholarly information. For example, they're aware that Jesus didn't believe in the Trinity or the Hellfire doctrine. Scholars weren't always aware of that fact. That means Jehovah's Witnesses did their research. They're *very* well-versed in some of these biblical subjects. How are they unaware that 1 Timothy 2:12 and 1 Corinthians 14:34–35 are not original to Paul?[3]

Is the Watchtower Society unaware that the verses were added later, or is it uninformed about the Bible and early Christianity? Although they seem informed in other areas, I can only assume they intentionally ignore the Bible's history.

44. Why do women have to wear hijabs in some cases?

Jehovah's Witnesses base their hijab doctrine on 1 Corinthians 11:11–15:

> Nevertheless, in the Lord woman is not independent of man or man independent of woman. For just as woman came from man, so man comes through woman; but all things come from God. Judge for yourselves: is it proper for a woman to pray to God with her head unveiled? Does not nature itself teach you that if a man wears

long hair, it is degrading to him, but if a woman has long hair, it is her glory? For her hair is given to her for a covering.

1 CORINTHIANS 11:11–15

This Bible verse seems to imply that women are equal to men. It also seems to say that women should wear a veil when they *pray*. Why do Jehovah's Witnesses insist women wear head coverings when leading the congregation in some way?

The verse also implies that the veil is the woman's hair. Is the verse saying that women should have long hair and men should have short hair? Should women wear a hijab only if they have short hair?

Of course, the governing body will provide us with all of this information. They have an excellent track record of correctly inter-preting the Bible—if we ignore their hundreds of mistakes.

CHAPTER 6
SHUNNING

45. Why do Jehovah's Witnesses mandate that members shun people? Why is it codified in their rules?

The Watchtower Society justifies its shunning policy with the following verse:[1]

But now I am writing to you not to associate with anyone who bears the name of brother or sister who is sexually immoral or greedy, or is an idolater, reviler, drunkard, or robber. Do not even eat with such a one.

1 CORINTHIANS 5:11

Paul wrote that letter to the congregation in Corinth. A man in the congregation had slept with his stepmother and was bragging about it in church. Paul instructed the Corinthian congregation to shun the man for his behavior, fearing it would make the early Christian church look bad.[2]

The Corinthian congregation responded negatively to Paul's

command. They shunned the man but, in the process, discovered that shunning is deeply painful. Human beings are simply not supposed to shun other humans. In response, Paul sent another letter to the Corinthian congregation and reversed his shunning policy.

> But if anyone has caused pain, he has caused it not to me, but to some extent—not to exaggerate it—to all of you. This punishment by the majority is enough for such a person; so now instead you should forgive and console him, so that he may not be overwhelmed by excessive sorrow.
>
> *2 CORINTHIANS 2:5–7*

Why do Jehovah's Witnesses selectively choose to read Paul's first letter to the congregation in Corinth but completely ignore his response? How can they justify the excessive sorrow they spread to thousands of shunned ex-members?

46. Did Jehovah's Witnesses lie on their website and in a Norway courtroom by claiming that the religion does not mandate shunning?

One Jehovah's Witness article titled "Do Jehovah's Witnesses Shun Those Who Used to Belong to Their Religion?" heavily implies they don't shun people:[3]

> Those who were baptized as Jehovah's Witnesses but no longer preach to others, perhaps even drifting away from association with fellow believers, are not shunned. In fact, we reach out to them and try to rekindle their spiritual interest.

That conveniently says nothing about disfellowshipped people.

This paragraph is about inactive people who've stopped going in service. Why didn't they unequivocally denounce shunning as an evil practice that is never done in any form by Jehovah's Witnesses? They go on to address disfellowshipped people a few paragraphs down:

> Disfellowshipped individuals may attend our religious services. If they wish, they may also receive spiritual counsel from congregation elders. The goal is to help each individual once more to qualify to be one of Jehovah's Witnesses. Disfellowshipped people who reject improper conduct and demonstrate a sincere desire to live by the Bible's standards are always welcome to become Jehovah's Witnesses again.

Are Jehovah's Witnesses ashamed of their practice of shunning? Why aren't they stating plainly what God supposedly instructed them to do? The elder's handbook has a list of disfellowshipping offenses. Chapter 12, paragraph 17, subsection 1 of the *Shepherd the Flock of God Elder's Manual*, 2021 edition, says the following:

> Unnecessary Association With Disfellowshipped or Disassociated Individuals: Willful, continued, unnecessary association with disfellowshipped or disassociated nonrelatives despite repeated counsel would warrant judicial action.

The elder's handbook clearly lists conditions under which Jehovah's Witnesses should be shunned. Even if this isn't explicitly stated in the handbook, it's widely practiced culturally. Additionally, the Watchtower Society encourages an alarming view of outsiders.

47. Why does the Watchtower Society teach that anybody critical of the religion to any degree is mentally diseased?

A 2011 *Watchtower* clearly outlines how Jehovah's Witnesses are supposed to feel about anybody critical of the religion. That includes me, and that now includes you after having read this book:

> The Bible says that apostates are mentally diseased and that they use their teachings to make others think like them. (1 Timothy 6:3, 4) Jehovah is like that good doctor. He clearly tells us to stay away from false teachers. We must always be determined to follow his warning.
>
> JEHOVAH'S WITNESSES. *THE WATCHTOWER, STUDY ED. (SIMPLIFIED)*. JULY 15, 2011. P. 11

What kind of atmosphere does the Watchtower Society think they're fostering by saying that to their members? How can they justify brazenly twisting the truth by claiming they don't shun?

48. Why do Jehovah's Witnesses forbid members from attending the funeral or wedding of a friend or family member who isn't a Jehovah's Witness?

This rule falls under the apostasy category, which refers to participation in interfaith activities. Why is it a disfellowshipping offense, as outlined in the Elder's Handbook, *Shepherd the Flock of God?*

49. Why did Jehovah's Witnesses release a *Watchtower* article condemning shunning in 1947 and subsequently codify the practice in 1952?

Jehovah's Witnesses released Awake! in 1947, which talks about excommunication. It says the following:[4]

If you are one of the 138,000,000 people in the world that were born and raised as "Protestants," then you are already excommunicated by the Roman Catholic Hierarchy. This means that you are looked upon with the blackest contempt by the Vatican, being cursed and damned with the Devil and his angels.

JEHOVAH'S WITNESSES. "ARE YOU ALSO EXCOMMUNICATED?" *AWAKE!.* JANUARY 8, 1947, P. 27

The organization seemed to understand why shunning was so damaging five years before implementing it. If Jehovah's Witnesses were picked as Jesus' chosen organization in 1919, why did Jesus inspire them to release anti-shunning material up to 1947?

50. Why did Jehovah's Witnesses defend and speak highly of Freemasons in 1947?

Jehovah's Witnesses also seemed to defend Freemasons in the 1947 *Awake!* article on ex-communication:

All those belonging to such lodges as the Masonic, Fenians, Independent Order of Good Templars, Odd Fellows, Sons of Temperance, or the Knights of Pythias, are also excommunicated.

What changed? Jehovah's Witnesses were supposedly chosen by Jesus as his representative on earth in 1919. Why did they both defend Freemasonry and condemn shunning after being selected by Jesus? Is Jehovah unsure of his feelings on any given subject? If He changed His mind about which organization should represent him, would that organization tell us?

51. Why is selling lottery tickets at a gas station a disfellowshipping offense?

I understand that Jehovah's Witnesses aren't allowed to smoke cigarettes, chew tobacco, or play the lottery. I don't understand why they aren't allowed to work in a position where they would be expected to sell those items to people. Just how divorced from society should we be, according to Jesus? Is it okay to be in a store where cigarettes are sold?

Is it okay for a Jehovah's Witness to invest in the stock market, knowing that some of the money they make will come from Philip Morris, the cigarette company? It's unacceptable to make any money from tobacco sales. Why do Jehovah's Witnesses earn revenue from the H. M. Riley Trust, which is invested in cigarette companies?[5]

52. Why are cannabis gummies banned in legal areas, but alcohol is not banned?

Cannabis is arguably less harmful than alcohol by a wide margin. Consuming anything through combustion, like smoking a cigarette, can be very damaging to a person's health. However, consuming cannabis gummies is not using combustion and is not damaging to a person's health in any way. Why is alcohol allowed, but cannabis within legal states and countries is not?

53. Why is it a disfellowshipping offense to get remarried after divorcing an abusive partner unless that partner cheated?

As a young Jehovah's Witness myself, I had to deal with a terribly abusive father. My mother left with me repeatedly, but the elders encouraged her to return. She wasn't allowed to remarry even when she finally permanently escaped from him. She was permanently linked to him. He had cheated on her years earlier, but she forgave him for it. After forgiving him, she wasn't allowed to leave.

My mother was stuck with my dad to the bitter end unless he cheated. Why do Jehovah's Witnesses command women and men to stay linked to abusive partners, no matter what?

54. Why are Jehovah's Witnesses so determined to prevent members from having outside relationships?

In their 2016 convention, Jehovah's Witnesses presented a video colloquially called "the Bunker Video." It portrays Jehovah's Witnesses sitting together in a locked basement, hiding from authorities. They're in the Great Tribulation. Each one tells a story about how they remained loyal to Jehovah.

One of the older women present tells a story about her coworkers. She said they were trying to be friendly with her. They invited her to get coffee with them. She took pride in the fact that she didn't give in to associating with them. She separated herself and stopped her friendly attitude.

Why do Jehovah's Witnesses view the outside world this way? Why is it important for the Society to prevent members from having outside friendships?

CHAPTER 7
PAGANISM

55. Why did Jehovah's Witnesses label shunning as a pagan practice in 1947?

The 1947 *Awake!* article is a perfect example of the organization's hypocrisy. They spent a fair bit of it opining about shunning practices. This *Awake!* Alone has sparked multiple questions I'd love to have answered by the leadership. The second column of the 1947 Awake! says shunning is of pagan origin. They make the same argument about Christmas.

Where, then, did this practice originate? The Encyclopaedia Britannica says that papal excommunication is not without pagan influence, "and its variations cannot be adequately explained unless account be taken of several non-Christian analogues of excommunication." The superstitious Greeks believed that when an excommunicated person died the Devil entered the body, and therefore, "in order to prevent it, the relatives of the deceased cut his body in pieces and boil them in wine."

There doesn't seem to be a citation for the quote from Encyclopedia Britannica. I have no idea if it accurately represents what was said in the 1947 edition.

56. What do Jehovah's Witnesses mean when they say "pagan?"

Jehovah's Witnesses have a long list of things that are banned for having pagan roots. As far as I can tell, "paganism" could mean anything. The Olympics are banned because the opening ceremony includes torch lighting, and the Olympics started in Greece. By that logic, anything that's not explicitly of Christian origin is pagan. Even explicitly Christian practices can have pagan roots in their eyes.

Here is a short list of things banned within the religion for having some ties to paganism. I'll be asking specific questions about some of these things later. As of when this book was published, the list stands as follows:[1]

- Christmas, Easter, birthdays, New Year's Eve, Valentine's Day, Mother's Day, Father's Day, Halloween, Dia de los Muertos (a Mexican tradition), and every other holiday for their own reasons
- Carnivals—Jehovah's Witnesses. *Awake!*. March 8, 1973, pp.5-8
- Olympics—Banned for the reasons mentioned above.
- Throwing Rice, Throwing the Bouquet, Wedding Marches
- Rosary, Star of David, Astrology
- Symbols on graves such as fish, anchor and dove, peacock
- Democracy
- Mazes and Labyrinths—Jehovah's Witnesses. *Awake!*. December 22, 1999. pp.20-24

- The Cross
- Jehovah's Witnesses think Jesus died on a stake driven into the ground instead of a cross.
- Hell
- Immortality of the Soul
- Jehovah's Witnesses think only angels and anointed people have immortal souls. Normal Jehovah's Witnesses will still be able to die after Armageddon.
- Clerical Celibacy, Trinity, Mary the mother of God, Saying "Bless you."
- Philosophy
- Specifically, Taoism, Confucianism, Greek Philosophy, Materialism, and Platonic philosophy.
- Throwing Soil into a grave, Throwing flowers into a grave.
- Drawing Halos on religious figures
- The Twist and certain other forms of dancing[2]

57. Why are some things acknowledged as pagan but acceptable anyway?

List of things that have pagan roots but are acceptable anyway:[3]

- Veil on bride
- Bridesmaids have the same color as the bride, or even white.
- Wedding Ring.
- The Watchtower Society acknowledges pagan roots, but they're deliberately ignored.
- Wedding cakes, Calendars, using flowers at a funeral.
- Piñatas.
- Piñatas aren't technically banned but heavily discouraged.

- Disfellowshipping.
- Originally believed to have pagan origins, the practice was implemented within five years of releasing an article condemning it as pagan.

Jehovah's Witnesses acknowledge that they believe the veil has a connection to paganism in a Watchtower from 1969:

To some in Germany, a white gown signifies virginity. Others there believe that it prevents evil spirits from recognizing the bride. In Japan, some view the white gown as a symbol of mourning; the bride 'dies' to her parents and remains with her husband until death.

JEHOVAH'S WITNESSES. *THE WATCHTOWER.*
JANUARY 15, 1969. PP. 57-61.

In the following sentence, they excuse the wedding veil as acceptable anyway. "However, to many persons throughout the earth, the white dress is simply a quaint tradition with no meaning. A Christian bride need not think that a white gown is essential, nor that it is universally forbidden."

58. Why is the Twist banned as a dance with pagan roots?

In the 1960s, there was a fear-mongering campaign over dancing. The fear swept through traditionalist communities the same way anti-LGBT sentiment has swept through modern traditionalist communities. Here's what Jehovah's Witnesses had to say about dancing:

Many of the news reports will likely have a few words about the origin of a new dance, and this is true of the twist. Time magazine, for instance, commented:

"The Twist at first was an innocent enough dance; it has since been largely discarded in favor of such refinements as 'The Roach' and 'The Fly.' But the youngsters at [a certain New York nightclub] [sic] have revived The Twist and parodied it into a replica of some ancient tribal puberty rite. The dancers scarcely ever touch each other or move either feet. Everything else, however, moves. The upper body sways forward and backward and the hips and shoulders twirl erotically, while the arms thrust in, out, up and down."

JEHOVAH'S WITNESSES. "HOW SHOULD CHRISTIANS VIEW DANCING?" *THE WATCHTOWER.* JULY 1, 1962. PP. 409–414

Later in the article, they use the Twist as an example of an unacceptable dance because of its connection to paganism.

In this example we have found that the dance craze mainly involves bodily gyrations and that the words used to describe them are "frantic," "sensual" and "erotic." You have also learned what kind of persons developed the dance and that it is basically an imitation of some pagan tribe's dance, involving gestures of a sexually suggestive nature.

59. Why are mazes and labyrinths labeled as pagan by Jehovah's Witnesses?

Mazes and labyrinths are also of pagan origin in the eyes of Jehovah's Witnesses. Here's a quote from a 1999 issue of the *Awake!*:

Large floor mazes were laid in other medieval French and Italian cathedrals and churches, including those at Amiens, Bayeux, Orléans,

Ravenna, and Toulouse. The one at Reims was destroyed 200 years ago, and the Mirepoix Cathedral's maze features a central Minotaur.

Regarding the incorporation of labyrinths into prominent religious buildings, one authority writes: "The pagan labyrinth was adopted by the medieval Christian church and adapted for its own use by including Christian symbolism in the design."

JEHOVAH'S WITNESSES. AWAKE!.
DECEMBER 22, 1999 PP.20-24

Based on this magazine, the mazes and labyrinths they describe are of Christian origin, not pagan. Why do Jehovah's Witnesses believe that things of Christian origin are pagan?

60. Why can't Jehovah's Witnesses celebrate birthdays?

Jehovah's Witnesses strictly forbid birthdays. Here are their reasons:

- Birthday celebrations have pagan roots.
- Early Christians didn't celebrate birthdays.
- Christians aren't required to celebrate birthdays.
- The Bible never refers to a servant of God celebrating a birthday.

Let's ask about each reason in detail.

61. Birthday reason 1: Why are pagan roots ignored for wedding rings or brides' veils, but not for birthday celebrations?

The first reason listed on Jehovah's Witnesses' website as to why they can't celebrate birthdays is because birthday celebrations have pagan roots.

When asked why Jehovah's Witnesses are allowed to wear wedding rings, which is another explicitly pagan practice, the response from the Watchtower Society was the following:

> Moreover, the wedding ring at one time had religious significance. Yet, most people today do not know that, considering a wedding ring a mere evidence that someone is married.

> JEHOVAH'S WITNESSES. *THE WATCHTOWER.*
> FEBRUARY 15, 2007. P. 30

Paganism is a problem for Jehovah's Witnesses, but only in certain circumstances. Jehovah's Witnesses addressed the "pagan roots" of wind chimes in a 1981 *Watchtower* article.

> If one's motive in putting up a wind chime has nothing to do with false religion, superstition or demonism, and there is little possibility of others getting the wrong impression regarding its use in the home, it is a simple matter for personal decision.

> JEHOVAH'S WITNESSES. "QUESTIONS FROM READERS." *THE WATCHTOWER.* JUNE 1, 1981.
> P. 31

According to that *Watchtower* passage, pagan roots aren't a problem for Jehovah's Witnesses if the intent is not to participate in a pagan practice and it's not perceived as pagan worship. Birthdays are not perceived as pagan worship. Additionally, as with wedding rings, the pagan roots of birthdays are so far removed from paganism that most people don't know they have pagan roots.

Again, what constitutes "pagan roots?" It now appears to be anything that isn't of Jehovah's Witness origin.

62. Birthday reason 2: We have no accounts of early Christians celebrating birthdays—So what?

The second reason listed on the Jehovah's Witness website for not celebrating birthdays is that early Christians didn't celebrate birthdays.

I'm not sure I understand the connection between what ancient people did or did not do and what we should be doing today. Ninety percent of ancient people were illiterate. Should modern Christians also mirror that aspect of culture and society?

63. Birthday reason 3: Christians aren't required to celebrate birthdays—So what?

The third reason listed for avoiding birthday celebrations is that Christians aren't required to celebrate them. They're only required to celebrate Jesus' death.

There are many things Christians aren't required to do, but they do them because they enjoy them. For example, Christians aren't required to keep cats in their homes, and the Bible doesn't require Christians to attend a religious service twice weekly. The lack of a requirement is not the same as a requirement *not* to do something.

64. Birthday reason 4: The Bible never refers to a servant of God celebrating a birthday—So what?

The fourth and final reason listed on the Jehovah's Witness website for refusing to celebrate birthdays is that the Bible never refers to a servant of God celebrating a birthday. Here's what the website said on the subject:

This is not simply an oversight, for it does record two birthday cele-brations by those not serving God. However, both of those events are presented in a bad light.

When I was a Jehovah's Witness, I was told it was because somebody lost a head at every birthday celebration mentioned in the Bible. That's a funny observation I hadn't noticed before, and it's effectively the logic being used in their fourth reason for avoiding birthdays.

I simply don't accept that justification. If that's the reason why Jehovah's Witnesses don't celebrate birthdays, then they shouldn't keep dogs, either. Every time the Bible mentions dogs, it's in a negative light.[4] Despite that fact, Jehovah's Witnesses aren't forbidden from keeping them. Jehovah's Witnesses' rules are unevenly applied.

65. Why is toasting at weddings banned for Jehovah's Witnesses?

Jehovah's Witnesses are banned from toasting at weddings because of—you guessed it—its possible connection to paganism.

A common practice at weddings and on other social occasions is toasting. The 1995 International Handbook on Alcohol and Culture says: "Toasting . . . is probably a secular vestige of ancient sacrificial libations in which a sacred liquid was offered to the gods . . . in exchange for a wish, a prayer summarized in the words 'long life!' or 'to your health!'

True, many people may not consciously view toasting as a religious or superstitious gesture. Still, the custom of lifting wine glasses heavenward might be viewed as a request to "heaven"—a superhuman force—for a blessing in a way that does not accord with that outlined in the Scriptures.

JEHOVAH'S WITNESSES. "CHAPTER 13:
CELEBRATIONS THAT DISPLEASE GOD".

KEEP YOURSELVES IN GOD'S LOVE. 2008.

Toasting, The Olympics, and carnivals are just as removed from paganism as wedding rings and wind chimes. Despite that, wind chimes and wedding rings are allowed while the others are not.

The Governing Body claims to receive guidance from God himself. They claim that the Watchtower Society has been Jesus' chosen representative on earth since 1919. Why would Jehovah apply rules unevenly?

66. Why do Jehovah's Witnesses believe Hell is of pagan origin?

Hell is a Christian creation, though Jesus didn't believe in it. Christianity didn't adopt it until hundreds of years later. Many believe our modern concept of Hell was shaped by Dante's poem "The Divine Comedy." The Christian concept of Hell was described in great detail in the book The Apocalypse of Peter, written around the same time as the Book of John.[5]

The words "apocalypse" and "revelation" mean the same thing in different languages. Apocalypse can also mean "explaining.". There was debate over whether the Apocalypse of John (the book of Revelation) or the Apocalypse of Peter should be in the Bible. Obviously, the Apocalypse of John won at the end of the day.

The Apocalypse of Peter contains graphic descriptions of Hell as the reader is taken on a tour to see the most horrific punishments imaginable. Some of those punishments include the following:

- Liars whose lies caused the death of martyrs have their lips cut off, with fire in their bodies and entrails.
- Rich people who neglected the poor are clothed in rags and pierced by a sharp pillar of fire.

- Women who had premarital sex have their flesh torn to pieces.
- Mothers who committed infanticide have their breast milk congeal into flesh-devouring animals that torment both parents (their dead children are delivered to a caretaking angel called Temlakos).

67. When Jehovah's Witnesses use the term "pagan," is it intended to apply to anything that's not of Jehovah's Witness origin?

Jehovah's Witnesses seem to believe that even things of Christian origin are of pagan origin. Just because non-Christians had a similar concept doesn't mean it was lifted directly from non-Christians. If it only applies to anything of non-Christian origin, why are the cross, Hell, mazes, and labyrinths banned?

CHAPTER 8
EVIL LEADERS

68. Why did Joseph Rutherford have a mansion built and deeded to Bible characters?

n 1929, Joseph Rutherford had a mansion built and deeded to Bible characters. It was named Beth Sarim, meaning House of Princes. He decided to stay in the mansion until the Bible characters arrived. You know, to keep it warm for them.

Finding out about this fact finally caused all of my doubts about the religion to coalesce. If there was any possible explanation for this besides greed and exploitation, I believe I would have found it already.

69. Why did Jehovah's Witnesses seemingly erase the mansion from their history?

Why did Jehovah's Witnesses remove mentions of Beth Sarim from their literature? Are they ashamed of their past? As of 1919, the Watchtower Society was Jesus' chosen organization on Earth.

Why would they be ashamed of anything that's happened since that point? If this was only a case of a man doing something selfish and hiding behind Jehovah's Witnesses, why hasn't he been denounced as a fraud, and had the doctrine he introduced reversed?

70. Why did the Watchtower Society still celebrate Christmas after being chosen by Jesus in 1919?

Was Jesus okay with Christmas at the time? Did he change his mind? For that matter, why did the Watchtower Society still use the cross at the time? Why were blood transfusions still acceptable? Are those things okay now, or were they wrong back then?

71. Why did Joseph Rutherford write a letter to Hitler endorsing his beliefs about Jews?

Jehovah's Witnesses are strictly forbidden from having any involvement in political matters. Why did Joseph Rutherford, the second president of the Watchtower Society, express his support for Hitler? The letter to Hitler and the supportive "Declaration of Facts" document were referenced in Jehovah's Witnesses' 1975 yearbook.[1]

The letter to Hitler expresses distinctly pro-German positions. Joseph Rutherford took a political stand and respected and admired Hitler.

Dear Reichskanzler,

   …

The Brooklyn headquarter of the Watchtower Society is pro German in an exemplary way and has been so for many years. For that reason, in 1918, the president of the Society and seven members of the board of directors were sentenced to 80 years in prison, because the president refused to use two of the magazines published in America under his direction for war propaganda against Germany. These two magazines, "The Watchtower" and "Bible Student" were the only magazines in America which refused to engage in anti-German propaganda and for that reason were prohibited and suppressed in America during the war.

RUTHERFORD, JOSEPH. *LETTER TO HITLER.*
1933

A few paragraphs down, the letter continued to put a puff in Hitler's petticoat.

The Bible Researchers of Germany are fighting for the very same high ethical goals and ideals which also the national government of the German Reich proclaimed respecting the relationship of humans to God, namely: honesty of the created being towards its creator.

RUTHERFORD, JOSEPH. *LETTER TO HITLER.*
1933

We don't even need to reference the Declaration of Facts or the letter to Hitler to see how Joseph Rutherford felt about Jews.

72. Why did Joseph Rutherford hate Jews so much?

In 1927, he published this statement in the Watchtower Society's publication *The Golden Age:*

Be it known once and for all that those profiteering, conscienceless, selfish men who call themselves Jews, and who control the greater portion of the finances of the world and the business of the world, will never be the rulers in this new earth. God would not risk such selfish men with such an important position.

JEHOVAH'S WITNESSES. *THE GOLDEN AGE.* FEBRUARY 23, 1927. P. 343

73. How can Jehovah's Witnesses believe that Jesus chose the Watchtower Society as his representative on earth while somebody as vile as Joseph Rutherford was in charge in 1919?

Why is this still doctrine? How could Jehovah's Witnesses possibly believe that Jesus picked Joseph Rutherford as the leader of his representation on earth?

74. Why lie about the reason Joseph Rutherford banned beards?

In December 2023, beards were unbanned for the first time since 1925. Governing Body member Stephen Lett spoke on the subject. He explained that beards were banned because they were associated with a rebellious political attitude.

Except that's not why they were banned. The real story is still available on the Jehovah's Witness website.[2] The story was originally told in 1971 by William J. Schnell in his book titled *30 Years a Watchtower Slave.* Four years later, Jehovah's Witnesses published the story in their 1975 yearbook.

Rutherford engaged in a fierce power struggle to regain control of the Watchtower Society from the Bible Students. When he won, he banned members from wearing beards to stamp out the challenge to his power.

An amusing incident took place at the time of the Judge's visit. The Director of our German branch, as had many before him, had grown a large beard, patterned after Charles T. Russell's beard. The Judge did not want anything at all to remain which might remind him of Russell—not even the cultivation of a beard. So, sitting at the table for dinner one night within my earshot, the Director asked the Judge for one more large rotary press. The Judge said nothing for a while, merely ate. So, suddenly he looked up, his eyes pinned severely on the Director's huge beard and said, "I will buy you the press if you take that thing off," pointing to the beard. It surely shocked the Director's sensibilities, but he meekly heeded the warning and soon shamefacedly appeared minus the beard.

SCHNELL, WILLIAM J. 30 YEARS A WATCHTOWER SLAVE. 1971. PP. 51–52

That story was told in Schnell's book in 1971. A similar story was told a few years later in the Jehovah's Witnesses' 1975 yearbook. Here's what their website says about it:

But more equipment was needed. For that reason Brother Balzereit asked Brother Rutherford for permission to buy a rotary press. Brother Rutherford saw the necessity and agreed, but on one condition. He had noticed that over the years Brother Balzereit had grown a beard very similar to the one that had been worn by Brother Russell. His example soon caught on, for there were others who also wanted to look like Brother Russell. This could give rise to a tendency toward creature worship, and Brother Rutherford wanted to prevent this. So during his next visit, within hearing of all the Bible House family, he told Brother Balzereit that he could buy the rotary press but only on the condition that he shave off his beard. Brother Balzereit sadly agreed and afterward went to the barber. During the next few days there were several cases of mistaken identity and some funny situations because of the "stranger" who was sometimes not recognized by his fellow workers.

JEHOVAH'S WITNESSES. *1974 YEARBOOK.* PP. 97–98

That's a little more charitable, but effectively the same situation. And again, it's still on their website. Why did Stephen Lett lie about the reason when it could be found on Watchtower Online Library?

Stephen Lett claimed it was because hippies wore beards and didn't want to be associated with a political movement. That was easily disproven by reading their website. The Watchtower Society claimed beards were banned because they wanted to prevent people from idolizing Charles Taze Russell. Why didn't they just ban that specific style of beard? If they're worried about creature worship, why do rooms in the headquarters have paintings of the Watchtower Society presidents? Isn't that a clearer example of idolatry? Either way, wearing a similar beard is mimicry, not idolatry. Did the Governing Body members or presidents between 1925 and 2023 not understand the difference?

75. Why do Jehovah's Witnesses pretend Joseph Rutherford's beard ban event didn't happen, even though it can be found on their website today?

Why aren't the Governing Body members just honest about their past? In the 2023 annual meeting, Jeffrey Winder described the process of changing doctrine. The Governing Body has the research staff dig up everything the Watchtower Society has ever said on a subject. The Governing Body then debates the issue. Doctrine changes if the decision is unanimous.

76. Did Stephen Lett lie when he claimed beards were banned because of their association with a rebellious political attitude?

Did the Governing Body's research staff overlook the story in the 1974 yearbook? Is the Governing Body genuinely completely oblivious to the *real* reason why beards were banned? Did they just make up a reason when reversing the decision? Why would they make up a reason rather than being honest with their members?

77. Why do Jehovah's Witnesses believe the United Nations is the Great Beast of Revelation? By whose authority do they make that declaration?

If we examine the Bible verses used by Jehovah's Witnesses to determine that the UN is the Great Beast, many other organizations or people could fit the bill. Why didn't Jehovah's Witnesses pick the European Union instead?

78. Why was the Watchtower Society registered as an NGO of the United Nations from 1992 to 2001?

Jehovah's Witnesses believe the United Nations to be the Great Beast of Revelation. They believe the UN will destroy religion during the Great Tribulation.

The Watchtower Society agreed to the UN pledge to uphold the goals and interests of the United Nations.

When The Guardian caught the Watchtower Society, it denied that it had agreed to the pledge. It claimed that the pledge wasn't on the application form when they joined when, in fact, it was.[3]

79. Why did the Watchtower Society pull out of the United Nations within days of *The Guardian* news article being published? Were they ashamed?

The Watchtower Society claims their writing staff registered the Watchtower Society as an NGO to gain access to the UN library, but the same books were available without being registered as an NGO of the United Nations.

CHAPTER 9
DEADLY DECISIONS

80. Why are blood transfusions banned for Jehovah's Witnesses?

Jehovah's Witnesses base their blood transfusion doctrine on one specific verse in the Old Testament. The verse is in Leviticus, which is part of the Old Law that Christians *aren't* required to follow.

And anyone of the people of Israel, or of the aliens who reside among them, who hunts down an animal or bird that may be eaten shall pour out its blood and cover it with earth.

For the life of every creature—its blood is its life; therefore I have said to the people of Israel: You shall not eat the blood of any creature, for the life of every creature is its blood; whoever eats it shall be cut off.

LEVITICUS 17:13–14

81. Why do Jehovah's Witnesses follow the old law regarding blood but ignore it regarding shellfish and pork?

Jehovah's Witnesses believe the old law was fulfilled and no longer necessary when Jesus came to earth. Why did they pick that one verse out of Leviticus and decide to follow it? Why do they ignore all the rest?

82. Why do Jehovah's Witnesses interpret the phrase "don't eat blood" as "don't take a lifesaving medical treatment?"

The word used in the Bible literally means "to eat." I thought using the word "eat" was an odd choice, so I looked deeper. The Hebrew word looks like this: "אָכְלְיו" It's pronounced 'ō·ḵə·lāw.

The word means explicitly to eat, to devour through your mouth and into your stomach. It doesn't relate to using blood in a lifesaving medical procedure. Why did Jehovah's Witnesses interpret the word as "to use in a medical procedure" instead of what it really means? Isn't that changing the Bible?

83. If God is all-knowing, why didn't he have Jesus mention blood transfusions even once?

The concept of a blood transfusion didn't exist when the book of Leviticus was written. However, God is all-knowing and all-wise. Why didn't Jesus mention it at least once if he wanted us to avoid blood transfusions? Wasn't Jesus sent to earth to set the standard for how the Christian religion is supposed to operate? Couldn't Jesus have condemned using blood in medical procedures specifically? That would have made it pretty clear.

84. Did the fourth president of the Watchtower Society, Fred Franz, ban blood transfusions to get attention?

After Joseph Rutherford's death, Nathan Knorr became the Watchtower Society president in 1942. Fred Franz became Knorr's vice president in 1945 and remained vice president until he became president in 1977.

In 1994, Jerry Bergman wrote a book about the history of objections to blood transfusions. Transfusions were heavily discouraged starting in 1945 and fully banned by 1961.

> After the Judge's [Joseph Rutherford's] death, as World War II was ending and persecution against the Witnesses began declining, along with the attendant drop in news-media publicity, Hayden C. Covington told the author [of THE FOUR PRESIDENTS] that Fred Franz saw the prohibition against blood transfusions as a way to accomplish two things: to continue to publicize the religion, and to create an uproar in the community.This reaction would convince the membership they were being "persecuted" and "suffering for righteousness sake," a sure sign they were "in the truth."

> BERGMAN, JERRY. *BLOOD TRANSFUSIONS: A HISTORY AND EVALUATION OF THE RELIGIOUS, BIBLICAL, AND MEDICAL OBJECTIONS.* 1994. P. 5

85. Why was it acceptable to receive an organ transplant from 1949 to 1961?

Jehovah's Witnesses allowed organ donation in 1949 but seemed to have a very strange view of the process.

> Have your teeth or hair fallen out? Has arthritis frozen your joints? Have a hole in your skull that needs plugging up? Need a new roof in your mouth? Or do you need a replacement for your lungs, kidneys or heart? If so, you will be interested to know that there are many shops around the country that are now in the business of

supplying "spare parts" for the human body, both natural and artificial.

JEHOVAH'S WITNESSES. AWAKE!.
DECEMBER 22, 1949. P.17

I didn't know they were doing roof-of-mouth transplants in 1949.

86. Why did the Watchtower Society decide that organ donation was a conscience matter in 1961?

Determining that a procedure or behavior is a conscience matter is a subtle way of telling members not to do it without explicitly stating it. Dating an outsider, having non-Jehovah's Witness friends, and taking certain medicines produced with blood fractions are all considered conscience matters.

The Watchtower Society listed organ donation as a "conscience matter" in 1961. It's not technically wrong, but it's very questionable. "God might decide to kill you in Armageddon. We just don't know." Look at the 1961 *Watchtower* article on the subject:

Is there anything in the Bible against giving one's eyes (after death) to be transplanted to some living person?-L. C., United States. The question of placing one's body or parts of one's body at the disposal of men of science or doctors at one's death for purposes of scientific experimentation or replacement in others is frowned upon by certain religious bodies. However, it does not seem that any Scriptural principle or law is involved. It therefore is something that each individual must decide for himself.

JEHOVAH'S WITNESSES. "QUESTIONS FROM

READERS." *THE WATCHTOWER.* AUGUST 1,
1961. P. 480

Reading these words would certainly be enough to prevent many Jehovah's Witnesses from getting organ donations. "The new system" is a term used by Jehovah's Witnesses to refer to where they believe they'll go after Armageddon. 144,000 anointed Jehovah's Witnesses go to heaven; every other Jehovah's Witness goes to a kind of Garden of Eden 2.0—the new system.

How many Jehovah's Witnesses needlessly died because they rejected organ donations for fear they wouldn't make it into the new system?

87. Why did the Watchtower Society ban organ donation in 1967, claiming that it's tantamount to cannibalism?

In 1967, the Watchtower Society released an article explicitly condemning organ donation as scripturally wrong. They said it was tantamount to cannibalism.

Sustaining one's life by means of the body or part of the body of another human...would be cannibalism, a practice abhorrent to all civilized people...It is not our place to decide whether such operations are advisable from a scientific or medical standpoint...Christians who have been enlightened by God's Word do not need to make these decisions based simply on the basis of personal whim or emotion. They can consider the divine principles and use these in making personal decisions as they look to God for direction, trusting him and putting their confidence in the future that he has in store for those who love him.

JEHOVAH'S WITNESSES. *THE*

WATCHTOWER. NOVEMBER 15, 1967. PP. 702–
704

If the number of Jehovah's Witnesses who died for rejecting an organ donation was high before, it certainly spiked dramatically after it moved from "conscience matter" to outright ban. Why did Jehovah change his mind? According to Jehovah's Witnesses, he's all-knowing, all-wise, and never changing.

88. Why did the Governing Body change the organ donation policy *again* in 1980?

The Watchtower Society once again reversed course in 1980.

There is no Biblical command pointedly forbidding the taking in of other human tissue. It is a matter for personal decision.

JEHOVAH'S WITNESSES. *THE WATCHTOWER.*
MARCH 15, 1980. P. 31

Will there ever be an apology for people who needlessly died between the years of 1961 and 1967 when it was banned?

89. Why did Jehovah's Witnesses believe that the recipients of an organ donation inherited the personality of the donator in 1975?

The 1975 *Watchtower* had this to say about organ donation five short years before it was unbanned again:

A peculiar factor sometimes noted is a so-called 'personality trans-plant.' That is, the recipient in some cases has seemed to adopt certain personality factors of the person from whom the organ came.

JEHOVAH'S WITNESSES. *THE WATCHTOWER.*
SEPTEMBER 1, 1975, P. 519

Why did Jehovah's Witnesses claim that people could inherit the personality of people from whom organs were donated? Where is the basis for this idea in the Bible?

CHAPTER 10
CHILD ABUSE

90. Why aren't elders explicitly instructed to call the police when they find out about a possible case of child sexual abuse?

Since the 1960s, involving secular authorities in anything has been frowned upon socially. The codified rules have fluctuated in many ways, but the culture dictates much of Jehovah's Witnesses' lives. To this day, no official instructions have been given to the elders to involve authorities when an assault occurs. As I show in the next question, the current handbook recommends elders "neither encourage nor discourage" parents from calling the police.

91. Why are elders instructed to work closely with the police in some circumstances but not others?

The elder's handbook instructs elders to meet with local police in case of a fire or burglary.

Communication with Local Law Enforcement: The elders should have up-to-date phone numbers for the police. Two elders (or a capable ministerial servant along with one elder) should be designated to visit the police station to promote good relations, expressing appreciation for their assistance if called upon. It may be advisable to ask the local authorities for security suggestions. Where several congregations are in the vicinity of the same police station, there should be good coordination as to how this contact with the police will be maintained.

JEHOVAH'S WITNESSES. ADDENDUM TO SHEPHERD THE FLOCK OF GOD ELDER'S HANDBOOK. 2022. P. 11, PARA. 26

Why are Jehovah's Witnesses explicitly instructed to connect with police in that case, but they aren't explicitly instructed to call the police in cases of child sexual abuse?

Child abuse is a crime. Never suggest to anyone that they should not report an allegation of child abuse to the police or other authorities. If you are asked, make it clear that whether to report the matter to the authorities or not is a personal decision for each individual to make and that there are no congregation sanctions for either decision. Elders will not criticize anyone who reports such an allegation to the authorities. If the victim wishes to make a report, it is his or her absolute right to do so.

JEHOVAH'S WITNESSES. "CHAPTER 12: CHILD ABUSE". SHEPHERD THE FLOCK OF GOD. SECTION 18–21, PP. 131–133

I appreciate that they eventually inserted that final line in the 2021 edition of the Elder's handbook. Next, I'd love it if they instructed elders to call the police. If the elders aren't instructed, maybe parents should be mandated to do so. Ambiguous language like this has allowed loopholes to be exploited over the years.

92. Does the Watchtower Society think that indoctrinating children is okay?

Jehovah's Witnesses have a series of children's cartoons called Caleb and Sophia. The cartoons teach children to be Jehovah's Witnesses. Why do Jehovah's Witnesses indoctrinate children instead of letting them choose their religion freely?

Do Jehovah's Witnesses believe that children are capable of fully grasping the consequences of their actions at 12 years old? If not, why would they allow children as young as eight to be baptized, effectively signing a lifelong contract with the Society?

93. Why does the Watchtower Society encourage children to get baptized as young as possible?

Do Jehovah's Witnesses think children can understand the consequences of signing a lifelong contract? Would Jehovah's Witnesses believe it's acceptable for two 12-year-olds to be married? If not, why do they think baptism, a much more serious decision, is acceptable?

CHAPTER 11
WRATH AND HATE

94. Why do Jehovah's Witnesses judge people?

Romans 2 condemns judging people. It clearly states that God will judge what's in people's hearts. Nobody on earth has the authority to fill that role in God's place.

Therefore you have no excuse, whoever you are, when you judge others; for *in passing judgement on another you condemn yourself,* because you, the judge, are doing the very same things. You say, "We know that God's judgement on those who do such things is in accordance with truth." Do you imagine, whoever you are, that when you judge those who do such things and yet do them yourself, you will escape the judgement of God?

ROMANS 2:1–4

95. Why don't Jehovah's Witnesses exercise patience and kindness?

Romans 2:4-5 says that God shows patience and kindness to people to bring them back to the fold.

Do you imagine, whoever you are, that when you judge those who do such things and yet do them yourself, you will escape the judgement of God? Or do you *despise the riches of his kindness and forbearance and patience*? Do you not realize that God's *kindness is meant to lead you to repentance*? But by your hard and impenitent heart you are *storing up wrath for yourself on the day of wrath*, when God's righteous judgement will be revealed.

ROMANS 2:1–5

Why do Jehovah's Witnesses think that shunning people is an effective way of bringing people back into the fold? Why do they completely ignore Romans 2:1–5 and show wrath and judgment anyway?

96. Why are Jehovah's Witnesses excited at the thought of critics being snuffed out like a flame?

Ex-Governing Body member Tony Morris gave a public talk about apostates. After describing a vivid scene where their bodies will burn and whatever doesn't burn will be eaten by maggots, he says the following:

Not a pleasant sight. But, what a fitting picture of the final end of all of god's enemies. Sobering, yet something we look forward to. However, the apostates and the enemies of Jehovah would say, "oh, that's gruesome. That's despicable. You teach your people these things?" No, *God* teaches *his* people these things. This is what he's foretelling. And frankly, for friends of Jehovah God, how reassuring, that they're finally going to be gone—all these despicable enemies that have just reproached Jehovah's name—destroyed, never ever to live again. Now, it's not that we rejoice in someone's death, but when it comes to god's enemies...finally, they're out of the way. Especially these despicable apostates who at one point had dedicated their life to god and then...they joined forces with Satan the Devil, the chief apostate of all time.

He quotes from a Bible verse next. He says,

But the wicked will perish. The enemies of Jehovah will vanish like glorious pastures. Particularly, they will vanish like smoke. So...I thought this would be a nice memory aid [to help] this verse stay in the mind. Here's what Jehovah is promising.

He lights a match, holds it in front of him for a moment, and blows it out. He looks back up from the match and smiles as he chuckles. The crowd laughs.

He says, "That's Jehovah's enemies. They're going to vanish like smoke."

Are these the actions of a godly man? Would Jesus ever be excited at the thought of a single person suffering, as Tony Morris did in his film about apostates?

97. Why do Jehovah's Witnesses *hate* gay people?

Jehovah's Witnesses would deny this charge. "We don't hate gay people," they say, "we love everybody. We just want them to meet God's moral expectations." We've already spoken about God's moral expectations, but I claim that Jehovah's Witnesses *do hate* gay people. Look at this quote from a 1995 *Awake!*

A youth who desires to please God must therefore conform to His moral standards and shun immoral behavior, though doing so may be agonizingly difficult. True, some individuals may very well be prone to homosexuality, just as some individuals are, according to the Bible, "prone to wrath." (Titus 1:7) But the Bible still condemns displays of unrighteous anger. (Ephesians 4:31) Similarly, a Christian cannot excuse immoral behavior by saying he was "born that way." Child molesters invoke the same pathetic excuse when they say their craving for children is "innate." But can anyone deny that their sexual appetite is perverted? So is the desire for someone of the same sex.

> JEHOVAH'S WITNESSES. "WHY DO I HAVE THESE FEELINGS?" *AWAKE!* FEBRUARY 8, 1995, P. 16

Jehovah's Witnesses view gay people the same way they view child molesters. They view them as morally depraved, dangerous to everybody around them, and believe that "their sexual appetite is perverted." Gay people wouldn't exist in a government set up and controlled by Jehovah's Witnesses. If that's not hate, I don't know what is. They can claim they don't hate them all they want, but it's a hard conclusion to avoid.

98. Why isn't it a disfellowshipping offense for a parent to abandon their children?

The Catholic Church controlled entire towns centuries ago. If a member of the town broke a Catholic rule, they wouldn't be able to rent a room anymore. They couldn't buy food or hang out with friends. The hope was that they would wander into the woods and die. Excommunication, or disfellowshipping, effectively marks a person as dead in the eyes of the shunners.

That is the punishment for being gay. That's the punishment for being critical of the religion, having a girlfriend, or smoking a cigarette. It's the punishment for a nearly endless list of supposed "sins."

When I was disfellowshipped in eleventh grade, my mother kicked me out of my home, and I had to drop out of high school. Jehovah's Witnesses seemed to think my mother made the right decision. Not only was she not punished, but her status and respect within the congregation seemed to rise.

Why is abandoning a child not viewed negatively? Why isn't it a disfellowshipping offense? Forget Jehovah's Witnesses' false claims that they don't shun. Why don't they ban shunning? If they're so desperate to convince the outside world that this isn't part of their core doctrine, why not guarantee it doesn't happen by creating a mandate?

99. Why do Jehovah's Witnesses have wrath in their hearts rather than love?

My last conversation with my mother ended with her telling me I was repulsive to her because I was critical of the Watchtower Society. After being kicked out of my house in eleventh grade, I was taken in by a Methodist woman named Sue. She was my daughter's great-grandmother.

Sue knew I believed in Jehovah's Witnesses doctrine, but she loved me anyway. When I realized that Jehovah's Witnesses were wrong and walked away from the whole thing, Sue still loved me. When I became addicted to heroin to cope with the loss of everything I ever knew, Sue let me live with her. When I was too destitute to buy Christmas presents for my own wife and daughter, Sue bought presents for them, addressed from me.

Sue never called me repulsive. No matter how low I got, she was still with me. Even after divorcing her granddaughter, she allowed me to live with her and loved me as if I were her own son. She was the perfect embodiment of the qualities Jesus expected from his followers. She took care of the poor and loved everybody, no matter what. Sue was my real mother, for all intents and purposes.

Sue died on September 21, 2022. She had nothing but love in her heart.

Every Jehovah's Witness I've ever known has disowned me. They look at me with disgust. They even call me repulsive. They hate me. They persecute me. They do not follow Jesus' example as Sue did.

Why do Jehovah's Witnesses have hate and wrath in their hearts instead of love, as Jesus commanded? Why do they pretend to love everybody while being selective about the love they show? How can someone claim to be a good person when the only love they ever show—even to their own children—is conditional? Why do they believe God will save them when they are the embodiment of the goats described in Jesus' sheep and goats parable in Matthew 25:31–46?

100. Why do Jehovah's Witnesses take good-faith criticism as a personal attack?

Criticism is how we all get better. How are we supposed to know God chooses the Governing Body if we can't point out the occasional flaw without being shunned? The Bible specifically instructs God's people to constantly question the leadership to ensure they speak for God (Deuteronomy 18:22). Does the Governing Body expect us to ignore that verse selectively?

––––––

We are each individually responsible for the decisions we make. Only God can judge (Romans 2:1–5). In that spirit, I will wait for

God's condemnation of my actions—not a group of men who obviously have a flawed interpretation of the Bible.

As Deuteronomy 18:22 instructs, I applied the test for a false prophet to the Watchtower Society. I've determined that they've spoken presumptuously, so I will no longer be frightened by them.

> If a prophet speaks in the name of the Lord but the thing does not take place or prove true, it is a word that the Lord has not spoken. The prophet has spoken it presumptuously; do not be frightened.

> *DEUTERONOMY 18:22*

NOTES

1. WORD TRANSLATION

1. Cooke, William. The Methodist New Connexion Magazine and Evangelical Repository, Volume XXXV., Third Series. 1867, p.493

2. FALSE PROPHECY

1. Grundy, Paul. "Facts about 607 B.C.E., 587 B.C. And Whether Jesus Started Ruling in 1914." Jwfacts.com, 2022, www.jwfacts.com/watchtower/607-587.php. Accessed 6 Jan. 2024.
2. Ehrman, Bart. "Background to Apocalypticism: The Maccabean Revolt | the Bart Ehrman Blog." The Bart Ehrman Blog, 2016, ehrmanblog.org/background-to-apocalypticism-the-maccabean-revolt/. Accessed 6 Jan. 2024.
3. "The Great Pyramid of Giza—Watchtower ONLINE LIBRARY." Jw.org, WOL, 2024, wol.jw.org/en/wol/d/r1/lp-e/1956362. Accessed 9 Jan. 2024.
4. Grundy, Paul. "Watchtower Quotes Regarding ..." Jwfacts.com, 2024, www.jwfacts.com/watchtower/quotes/20th-century-2000.php. Accessed 6 Jan. 2024.
5. Grundy, Paul. "1975 - Watchtower Quotes to Show What Really Was Predicted." Jwfacts.com, 2017, www.jwfacts.com/watchtower/1975.php. Accessed 2 Feb. 2024.

3. THE LGBT COMMUNITY

1. Siker, Jeff. "Homosexuality in the Bible (and the Christian Church) | the Bart Ehrman Blog." The Bart Ehrman Blog, 2019, ehrmanblog.org/homosexuality-in-the-bible-and-the-christian-church/. Accessed 3 Feb. 2024.
2. Siker, Jeff. "Homosexuality and the New Testament. Guest Post by Jeff Siker. | the Bart Ehrman Blog." The Bart Ehrman Blog, 2019, ehrmanblog.org/homosexuality-and-the-new-testament-guest-post-by-jeff-siker/. Accessed 3 Feb. 2024
3. "Am I Gay? Is It Wrong to Have Homosexual Urges? | Teenagers." JW.ORG, JW.ORG, 2024, www.jw.org/en/bible-teachings/teenagers/ask/pressure-to-be-gay/. Accessed 26 Jan. 2024.
4. "Why Don't Jehovah's Witnesses Celebrate Birthdays? | FAQ." JW.ORG, JW.ORG, 2024, www.jw.org/en/jehovahs-witnesses/faq/birthdays/. Accessed 3 Feb. 2024.

5. INCORRECT BELIEFS

1. Ehrman, Bart. "How Were People Crucified? | the Bart Ehrman Blog." The Bart Ehrman Blog, 2020, ehrmanblog.org/how-were-people-crucified/. Accessed 9 Jan. 2024.

2. "The King of the North" in the Time of the End | Watchtower Study. JW.ORG. Published 2020. Accessed January 6, 2024. https://www.jw.org/en/library/magazines/watchtower-study-may-2020/The-King-of-the-North-in-the-Time-of-the-End/

3. Ehrman, Bart. "The Non-Pauline Oppression of Women | the Bart Ehrman Blog." The Bart Ehrman Blog, 2020, ehrmanblog.org/the-non-pauline-oppression-of-women-for-members/. Accessed 3 Feb. 2024.

6. SHUNNING

1. Grundy, Paul. "Jehovah's Witnesses, Disfellowshipping and Shunning, Including Family Members." Jwfacts.com, 2015, www.jwfacts.com/watchtower/disfellowship-shunning.php. Accessed 9 Jan. 2024.

2. Ehrman, Bart. Paul and that Peculiar Church in Corinth | The Bart Ehrman Blog. The Bart Ehrman Blog. Published 2021. Accessed January 6, 2024. https://ehrmanblog.org/paul-and-that-peculiar-church-in-corinth/

3. Do Jehovah's Witnesses Shun Those Who Used to Belong to Their Religion?" JW.ORG, JW.ORG, 2024, www.jw.org/en/jehovahs-witnesses/faq/shunning/. Accessed 3 Feb. 2024.

4. Grundy, Paul. "Watchtower Quotes Regarding Pagan Practices." Jwfacts.com, 2016, www.jwfacts.com/watchtower/quotes/pagan-practices.php. Accessed 9 Jan. 2024.

5. "Henrietta M. Riley Trust - Jehovah's Witnesses." Jehovah's Witnesses, 18 Oct. 2022, avoidjw.org/donations/usa/hmrt/. Accessed 3 Feb. 2024.

7. PAGANISM

1. Grundy, Paul. "Watchtower Quotes Regarding Pagan Practices." Jwfacts.com, 2016, www.jwfacts.com/watchtower/quotes/pagan-practices.php. Accessed 20 Jan. 2024.

2. Jehovah's Witnesses. Watchtower. July 1, 1962, pp.409-414

3. Grundy, Paul. "Watchtower Quotes Regarding Pagan Practices." Jwfacts.com, 2016, www.jwfacts.com/watchtower/quotes/pagan-practices.php. Accessed 20 Jan. 2024.

4. Evans, Lloyd. "Traumatized by a Cupcake: The Latest Caleb & Sophia Monstrosity." YouTube, YouTube Video, 7 Jan. 2021, www.youtube.com/watch?v=e50ORAmICgA. Accessed 6 Jan. 2024.

5. Wikipedia Contributors. "Apocalypse of Peter." Wikipedia, Wikimedia Founda-

tion, 19 Jan. 2024, en.wikipedia.org/wiki/Apocalypse_of_Peter. Accessed 20 Jan. 2024.

8. EVIL LEADERS

1. Grundy, Paul. "Rutherford and the Watchtower's Support of Hitler." Jwfacts.com, 2015, www.jwfacts.com/watchtower/hitler-nazi.php. Accessed 6 Jan. 2024.
2. "Part 1—Germany—Watchtower ONLINE LIBRARY." Jw.org, WOL, 2024, wol.jw.org/en/wol/d/r1/lp-e/301974004#h=163. Accessed 24 Jan. 2024.
3. Grundy, Paul. "Watchtower Society - United Nations NGO Status 1992." Jwfacts.com, 2022, www.jwfacts.com/watchtower/united-nations-association.php#fn1. Accessed 6 Jan. 2024.